FOSTERING REGIONAL COOPERATION AND INTEGRATION FOR RECOVERY AND RESILIENCE

GUIDANCE NOTE

JANUARY 2022

ASIAN DEVELOPMENT BANK

ADB

Contents

Figure and Boxes

Abbreviations

ADB	Asian Development Bank
ASEAN	Association of Southeast Asian Nations
CAREC	Central Asia Regional Economic Cooperation
COVID-19	coronavirus disease
DMC	developing member country
fintech	financial technology
GMS	Greater Mekong Subregion
ICT	information and communication technology
ILO	International Labour Organization
MSMEs	micro, small, and medium-sized enterprises
OP7	Operational Priority 7 under Strategy 2030
RCI	regional cooperation and integration
SASEC	South Asia Subregional Economic Cooperation
SAARC	South Asian Association for Regional Cooperation
SDG	Sustainable Development Goal
UNESCAP	United Nations Economic and Social Commission for Asia and the Pacific

Executive Summary

Regional cooperation played an important role at the onset of the coronavirus disease (COVID-19) pandemic, bringing countries together to mitigate its spread and cushion its adverse consequences. As Asia and the Pacific begins to recover, regional cooperation will play an equal if not a more critical role in rebuilding smartly to inclusive, resilient, and sustainable economic revival. The challenges created by the pandemic are multifaceted, threatening to intensify poverty and inequality in the region and compounding climate change risks in complex ways. The path to recovery has opened many opportunities for collaboration among countries, building on their long experience in regional cooperation.

This guidance note provides a broad framework and identifies opportunities for fostering an inclusive, sustainable, and resilient recovery, where regional cooperation and integration (RCI) can supplement or complement national efforts. The publication advocates wider, deeper, and more open regional cooperation and integration.

- **Wider RCI** means expanding to new and emerging areas such as regional health security, trade in information and communication technology–enabled services, and financial safety nets, among others.

- **Deeper RCI** means diversifying within sectors or themes and taking a holistic approach through multistakeholder and multisectoral collaborations.

- **More open RCI** means adopting more fluid and flexible approaches to collaboration beyond existing subregional frameworks, enlarging the space for knowledge sharing and pooling knowledge and expertise.

The guidance note aims to help ADB developing member countries identify mutually beneficial initiatives in their transition to recovery; development partners harness the potential for operational complementarity; and the private sector contribute innovations in finance, knowledge, and practice. It complements ADB Strategy 2030's Operational Priority 7 (fostering RCI) by showing how its three pillars—greater and better connectivity, expanded global and regional trade and investment opportunities, and increased and diversified regional public goods—can be made more responsive to the evolving circumstances of economic recovery.

COVID-19 lockdown. A woman sits on the sidewalk in Lakeside Pokhara, Nepal during the pandemic that called off Visit Nepal 2020 (photo by Samir Jung Thapa).

1 Introduction

As the coronavirus disease (COVID-19) pandemic enters its second year, countries in Asia and the Pacific have begun to recover slowly despite recurring risks of infection by the virus and its variants. Although their paths to recovery will be different, all economies are aspiring to rebuild smartly toward recovery that is inclusive, sustainable, and resilient.

Regional cooperation was crucial in the pandemic's emergency phase; countries came together spontaneously to coordinate their responses through information sharing, cross-border trade and health protocols, surveillance and contact tracing, and pooling of financial resources, among others. Regional cooperation will be equally if not more critical as the Asia and Pacific region transitions from emergency to recovery. The Asian Development Bank (ADB) mandate on regional cooperation, enshrined in its Charter and operationalized in Operational Priority (OP7) of ADB's Strategy 2030, will confront a new and evolving landscape.

Issued in 2019 before the COVID-19 pandemic started, OP7 on fostering regional cooperation and integration (RCI) was structured around three strategic operational priorities or pillars: (i) greater and higher quality connectivity between economies, (ii) expanded global and regional trade and investment opportunities, and (iii) increased and diversified regional public goods. While the priorities remain relevant, they must broaden and deepen in response to the dramatic changes resulting from the pandemic as the region recovers. Modalities that deliver RCI assistance, including policy- and results-based lending, guarantees, public–private partnerships, and nonsovereign investment, must be more diverse.

This guidance note was prepared by ADB's RCI Thematic Group to show how the OP7 pillars can more quickly respond to the evolving circumstances of economic recovery. The guidance note advocates for wider, deeper, and more open RCI and identifies RCI opportunities in key emerging themes that underpin inclusive, sustainable, and resilient recovery. Although not exhaustive, the opportunities identified here can serve as starting points to guide ADB's developing member countries (DMCs) in catalyzing innovative ideas and approaches to collaboration. The guidance note's perspectives derive from ADB's more than 5 decades of RCI experience and expertise embodied in a wealth of knowledge products.

The guidance note has the following objectives:
(i) Provide the framework and principles for more responsive RCI in a milieu that has fundamentally changed in the aftermath of COVID-19.
(ii) Identify opportunities to foster inclusive, sustainable, and resilient recovery, where RCI can supplement or complement national efforts, and to leverage the experience of past and ongoing initiatives.
(iii) Broaden perspectives on innovative models of RCI institutional arrangements, governance, capacity development, and knowledge management that help achieve economic recovery.

The guidance note caters to a broad audience: governments; the private sector; development partners; and ADB's operations departments, including the Private Sector Operations Department and the Office of Public–Private Partnership. The guidance note is intended to be a companion piece to OP7. DMCs can use the guidance note to develop mutually beneficial regional initiatives that can complement national efforts to transition to recovery. The guidance note can be used to identify cooperation with development partners to harness the potential for operational complementarity based on additional financing, knowledge and expertise, and other institutional resources.[1] The opportunities identified in the guidance note suggest areas where the private sector can play an increasingly important role, including (i) technology and innovation as key drivers for recovery; (ii) innovative private sector finance for projects with regional cooperation themes; (iii) support for nascent sectors (e.g., privately funded care for the elderly); and (iv) cross-border business opportunities in agribusiness and for micro, small, and medium-sized enterprises (MSMEs) along economic corridors. For ADB's operations departments, the guidance note can help further sharpen the strategies, focus, and approaches of their RCI operations and country program strategies.

---

[1] ADB. 2019. *Strategy 2030 Operational Plan for Priority 7—Fostering Regional Cooperation and Integration 2019–2024*. Manila.

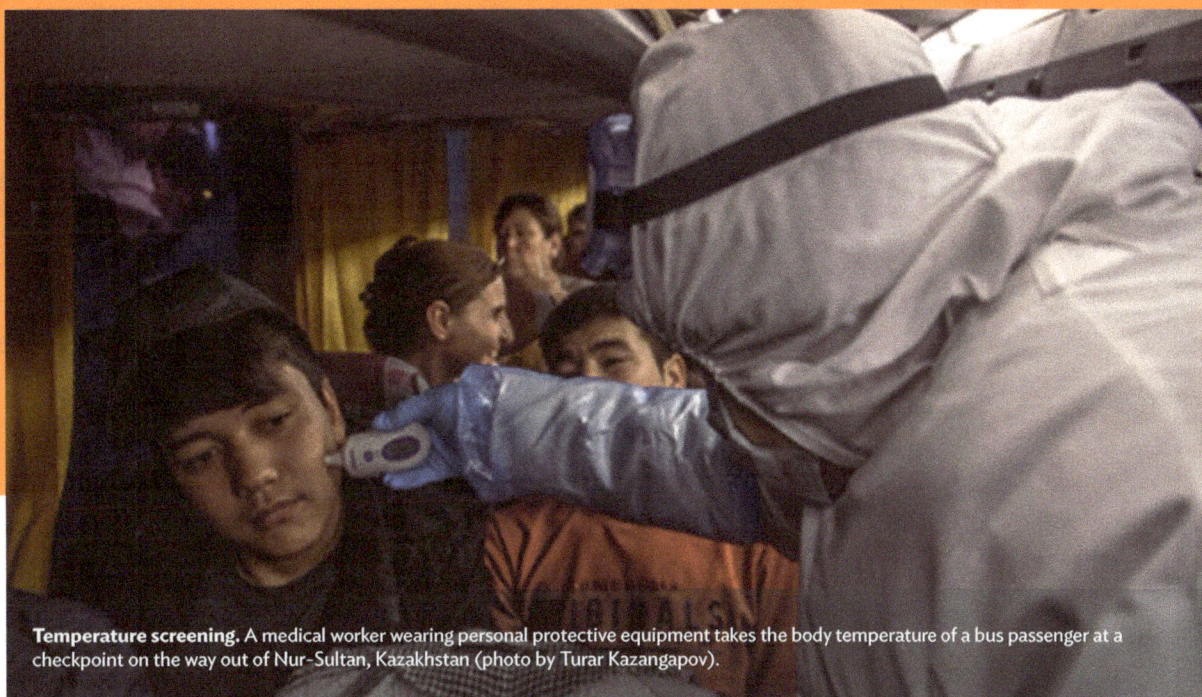

Temperature screening. A medical worker wearing personal protective equipment takes the body temperature of a bus passenger at a checkpoint on the way out of Nur-Sultan, Kazakhstan (photo by Turar Kazangapov).

2 Regional Cooperation and Integration Responses to COVID-19

Throughout Asia and the Pacific, noteworthy examples abound of prompt and sustained collaboration to mitigate the economic and social losses from the pandemic. Shortly after the World Health Organization announced in January 2020 that COVID-19 was a global health emergency, the South Asian Association for Regional Cooperation (SAARC) convened its first virtual summit on 15 March 2020 to coordinate the subregion's response to the crisis. India mobilized SAARC member countries to launch the COVID-19 Emergency Fund, to which SAARC members contributed. High-level health officials met shortly after the summit to initiate action on border protocols, people tracking, training, and electronic exchange of information. The Association of Southeast Asian Nations (ASEAN) introduced several initiatives to manage the crisis and ensure post–COVID-19 recovery. The Special ASEAN Summit in April 2020 created the COVID-19 ASEAN Response Fund to finance the procurement of medical equipment and supplies to fight the virus. The 37th ASEAN Summit in November 2020 adopted the Declaration on an ASEAN Travel Corridor Arrangement Framework to facilitate intra-ASEAN essential business travel while ensuring public health safety. The gathering endorsed the ASEAN Comprehensive Recovery Framework and its implementation plan, which will guide ASEAN's post–COVID-19 recovery.[2]

---

[2] The ASEAN Travel Corridor Arrangement Framework consists of five broad strategies: (i) enhancing the health system, (ii) strengthening human security, (iii) maximizing the potential of intra-ASEAN market and broader economic integration, (iv) accelerating inclusive digital transformation, and (v) advancing toward a more sustainable and resilient future.

The November 2020 Summit of ASEAN+3 (comprising ASEAN, the People's Republic of China, Japan, and the Republic of Korea) committed to work together to quell the pandemic and speed up recovery.

Subregional programs supported by ADB promptly and spontaneously responded to the pandemic. The Central Asia Regional Economic Cooperation (CAREC), Greater Mekong Subregion (GMS), and South Asia Subregional Economic Cooperation (SASEC) programs have taken initiatives to mitigate the pandemic, including coordinating intercountry movement of medical supplies and technical experts, pooling surveillance and contact tracing, and coordinating the planning and monitoring of COVID-response initiatives. Subregional platforms were used to conduct dialogue not only on control and mitigation measures but also on macro policies for economic recovery and the pandemic's impact on the poor and the vulnerable, women, migrant workers, and MSMEs. The GMS mobilized quick-disbursing funds to procure essential supplies and equipment at the onset of the pandemic. The GMS COVID-19 Response and Recovery Plan 2021–2023 was set in place.[3] CAREC established a health working group to implement the CAREC Health Strategy 2030 to promote health cooperation in strengthening national health systems; reinforce regional health security; and improve access to health services for migrants, mobile populations, and border communities. SASEC customs officials agreed to institute special regimes for sensitive and/or critical goods to keep borders open during the pandemic and develop an action plan for resiliency and preparedness to cope with emergencies. The Pacific Humanitarian Pathway on COVID-19 was established to expedite responses to humanitarian and health crises across the subregion[4] and is sustaining trade-related economic activities of MSMEs while ensuring gender equality.

In addition, ADB set up special facilities to provide resources that its DMCs could tap to support national and regional initiatives. On 13 April 2020, ADB established the COVID-19 Pandemic Response Option as part of ADB's $20 billion expanded assistance for DMCs' pandemic response. On 11 December 2020, ADB launched its $9 billion Asia Pacific Vaccine Access (APVAX) Facility, which has been helping promote safe, equitable, and effective access to vaccines across the region. ADB supported subregional initiatives to ensure the smooth flow of essential goods and services; strengthen infection surveillance, prevention, and control; and reduce disruptions to trade, investment, and mobility of people.

The challenges of the pandemic have reaffirmed that the response, prevention, and treatment of COVID-19 hinge on strong commitment and collaboration among countries. The region's decades-long practice and experience in RCI have enabled regional economies to pool their collective actions spontaneously and swiftly. Institutional mechanisms and cooperation frameworks already in place in different sectors expedited discourse and decision-making and the design and implementation of policies and initiatives.

---

3 The GMS COVID-19 Response and Recovery Plan 2021–2023 has three pillars: (i) promoting regional health security through the One Health approach; (ii) protecting the poor and vulnerable in border areas through job creation and safe and orderly movement of labor; and (iii) ensuring that borders remain open to facilitate transport and trade, rebuild agriculture, and generate safe and seamless tourism opportunities.
4 The Pacific Humanitarian Pathway on COVID-19 has supported the timely movement of medical supplies, technical experts, and humanitarian assistance to Pacific Islands Forum members.

Vaccinated worker. A garment worker goes back to work at a textile garment factory in Phnom Penh, Cambodia after her vaccination on 6 May 2021 (photo by Chor Sokunthea).

3 Key Challenges and Opportunities for Regional Cooperation and Integration

As the Asia and Pacific region transitions from emergency to recovery, the new economy will be fraught with uncertainties and vulnerabilities. The challenges before COVID-19—poverty, inequality, and climate change and disaster risks—will remain, but their ramifications will likely be more severe and solutions and responses to them more complex. In addition, the pandemic has spawned new challenges and opportunities:

(i) The interdependence brought about by globalization and connectivity, already threatened by rising waves of trade protectionism and economic nationalism even before the COVID-19 pandemic, has come under more intense pressure in the pandemic's aftermath.

(ii) Digitalization is rapidly changing the nature of work. Machines are taking over routine jobs, while technology is creating new jobs, altering old ones, and opening up opportunities. Recent years have seen the rise of the gig economy: a labor market characterized by the prevalence of short-term contracts and freelance work instead of permanent jobs. The development is challenging conventional approaches to building human capital through education; reshaping traditional perspectives on social protection; and prompting the revisiting of regulatory issues, such as the taxation of digital platforms.

(iii) COVID-19 has induced changes in work and consumer behavior that have prompted business to respond with models that rely heavily on digital platforms and solutions. The changes are generating cross-border demand for more secure private and public e-commerce and e-government services plus more accessible and reliable digital and information and communication technology (ICT) platforms for conducting digital trade.

(iv) Supply disruptions caused by the pandemic are accelerating changes in global and regional value chains that were already underway because of ongoing trade conflicts and the advent of the fourth industrial revolution. Strengthening trade integration through trade liberalization and trade facilitation can help regional economies navigate the shifting global value chain landscape. Regional cooperation among governments, working closely with the business sector, will be critical in fostering diversification and resilience in global value chains while keeping the benefits of international specialization.

(v) Compounding and cascading disaster risks have serious implications for a resilient and sustainable recovery as the current pandemic continues to collide with several other threats to human life. Compound hazards, which occur when multiple hazards take place simultaneously or one after another, have become prominent as countries manage climate and disaster risks while continuing to respond to the COVID-19 crisis. The impacts of climate change, including climate variation and more frequent and intense natural hazards, are increasing the complexity of the disaster "riskscape" across Asia and the Pacific.

(vi) Public debt has soared as governments try to cushion the impact of the pandemic, posing a risk to financial stability. An orderly exit strategy is needed to navigate the transition from extra stimulus to normal economic activity to ensure economic and financial stability.[5] Rising public debt will have serious implications for development finance and could threaten the viability of recovery and attainment of the Sustainable Development Goals (SDGs), which were already underfinanced even before COVID-19.

Despite the challenges, the region's growth has remained resilient since the pandemic's onset. Economic growth slumped during the first quarter of 2020 on account of cross-border trade disruptions, but the region slowly revived, with signs of recovery manifesting in the first half of 2021. The region found opportunities to build from the strengths it had acquired through the years. Asia and the Pacific has become the world's largest regional economy and has developed as a hub for trade and people flows. Global cross-border flows have been shifting to Asia in seven of eight dimensions: trade, capital, people, knowledge, transport, culture, resources, and the environment; the only flow that has declined is waste (environment).[6] The region is now home to half the world's people—workers, consumers, entrepreneurs, travelers—and is on the path to representing one-half of global gross domestic product. The region's share of the world's middle class is rising steadily.

The centrality of the region in the world economy has been bolstered in part through regional and subregional cooperation that forged closer economic links through infrastructure connectivity and trade and joint action on shared interests and goals. ADB-supported subregional initiatives—CAREC, GMS, and SASEC—have made significant progress in economic cooperation in various sectors. ADB has established strong partnerships and supported other subregional programs such as ASEAN, Brunei Darussalam–Indonesia–Malaysia–Philippines East ASEAN Growth Area, Bay of Bengal Initiative for Multi-Sectoral Technical and Economic Cooperation, Indonesia–Malaysia–Thailand Growth Triangle, Pacific Islands Forum Secretariat, and South Asian Association for Regional Cooperation. Future RCI can leverage these frameworks and partnerships to face the challenges and seize the opportunities of recovery expeditiously and effectively because of the goodwill developed through decades of collaboration.

---

5 B. Susantono, Y. Sawada, and C.Y. Park, eds. 2020. *Navigating COVID-19 in Asia and the Pacific*. Manila: ADB.

6 O. Tonby et al. 2019. The Future of Asia: Asian Flows Are Defining the Next Phase of Globalization. *Discussion Paper*. United States: McKinsey & Company.

Waiting for tourists. An antique carpet dealer in downtown Tbilisi is hopeful for tourism to revive (photo by Khatia Jijeishvili).

4 Rebuilding Smartly: Wider, Deeper, More Open Regional Cooperation and Integration

Fostering an inclusive, resilient, and sustainable recovery calls for stronger, more dynamic RCI. In the aftermath of COVID-19, RCI will need to be different and more compelling than it was before. It has to be wider, deeper, and more open to rebuilding smartly.

(i) **Wider RCI** involves expanding to new and emerging areas such as regional health security, gender and social protection, tourism and international safe travel, trade in ICT-enabled services, and trade in renewable energy, among others. Wider RCI involves focusing on the key enablers of recovery: digitization, skills and jobs, and financial sustainability.

(ii) **Deeper RCI** involves diversifying within sectors or themes, piloting and scaling up innovative approaches, taking a holistic approach through multi-stakeholder and multisectoral collaborations to inclusive and coordinated policy responses, and looking at institutional mechanisms and governance processes needed to operate seamlessly across national borders.

(iii) **More open RCI** involves adopting more fluid and flexible approaches to collaboration that cut across or go beyond the structural formalities of regional and subregional groupings to widen and deepen policy dialogues; enlarge the space for knowledge sharing and capacity development; and pool knowledge, expertise, and other resources more efficiently and effectively. More open RCI involves linking or aligning RCI initiatives with global, regional, and subregional frameworks and agendas, including the use of tool kits and guidelines where applicable, for greater efficiency, synergy, and impact. More open RCI endeavors reach out to new partners and thought leaders in the private sector, think tanks, academic institutions, and civil society organizations, while continuing to strengthen collaboration with traditional development partners.

The three RCI dimensions are not in silos. An RCI initiative can have the features of all three dimensions at the same time or move into each one gradually. The sequence is not set: an RCI initiative can start with any number of countries (more open RCI) that are willing to work together on a new theme or sector, for example, in the care sector[7] (wider RCI), by starting with information sharing and gradually taking on more complex activities, for example, a regional framework on unpaid work (deeper RCI).

Working along the three dimensions of a wider, deeper, and more open RCI will mean increasingly adopting a multisectoral, theme-based approach (rather than a single sector approach), and a multi-stakeholder approach involving subregional, national, and subnational partnerships; and developing, piloting, and scaling up innovative RCI models. The approaches will be underpinned by the One ADB approach stipulated in Strategy 2030, which supports the multidisciplinary, cross-sectoral, and transnational nature of the challenges that Strategy 2030 seeks to resolve. The approaches include (i) close collaboration between public and private sector operations staff on identifying and loosening bottlenecks that hinder development results, (ii) integrated solutions to incorporate advanced technologies with support from sector and thematic groups, and (iii) better research functions to strengthen the analytical base of operations and policy dialogue with clients.

Major themes where RCI could play an important role have emerged as critical to the recovery agenda. They present opportunities for widening, deepening, and opening up RCI in line with the three pillars of OP7 (see Figure). The themes will continue to evolve as the regional landscape unfolds during recovery.

Wider Regional Cooperation and Integration

(i) **Digitalization.** Already a trend before COVID-19, digitalization is expected to accelerate, enabling inclusive and sustainable recovery. Much will depend on government policies to bring down barriers to universal and affordable internet access, including inadequate physical infrastructure, inoperability between systems, and the lack of a supportive policy environment. Policies will need to tackle the dynamics of the digital economy that might give rise to technology-driven inequality, resulting in labor displacement; inability of the poor to access and use technological solutions; and lack of technological know-how to mitigate environmental degradation and disasters, which disproportionately affect the poor. Digital identification can help foster inclusive growth by unlocking access of consumers, workers, microenterprises, taxpayers and beneficiaries, civically engaged individuals, and asset owners to institutions.[8] Regional platforms can help countries better understand cross-border digitalization issues and challenges and policy responses to them. The major issues are basic data infrastructure, competition, innovation, access of micro businesses, and data privacy and cybersecurity.

---

[7] Care is an emerging sector, covering work in a variety of settings and across formal and informal economies. Some care is provided by health services, most of which is formal and public. Public services for childcare, early childhood education, disability and long-term care, and elder care comprise the care economy. Health, education, and social services overlap with other forms of paid and unpaid care given, for example, by family and community members, often because access to quality services is lacking (International Labour Organization. 2017. *The Care Economy*. Geneva).

[8] McKinsey Global Institute. 2019. *Digital Identification: A Key to Inclusive Growth*.

Figure: Opportunities for Wider, Deeper, and More Open Regional Cooperation and Integration in the Three Pillars of Strategy 2030's Operational Priority 7

	Greater and higher quality connectivity between economies		Global and regional trade and investment opportunities expanded	Regional public goods increased and diversified	
Wider regional cooperation and integration	**Digitalization** • Regional forums on challenges, issues, and policy responses to digitalization (competition, innovation access of micro businesses, data privacy, and cybersecurity) • Capacity building on digital solutions in different sectors **Education and Labor Markets** • Harmonization of technical and regulatory standards of data systems • Capacity building on applications of digital technologies in different sectors • Resource mobilization for technological development • Regional forums on challenges, issues, and policy responses to digitalization • Capacity building on digital solutions in different sectors	**Cross-Border Data Flows** • Regional mechanisms to streamline requirements for cross-border data flows • Regional cooperation to achieve last-mile connectivity in broadband infrastructure • Regionally consistent framework on cross-border data flows • Alignment with international standards and model laws **Financial Safety Nets** • Regional framework on safe international travel • Knowledge-sharing forum • Harmonized practices on contact tracing, risk classification, testing, mobile health insurance, and electronic travel certificates	**Supply Chains** • Engaging in deeper regional trade integration and stronger trade liberalization through mega-trade deals • Redirecting investments in the green and blue economy and in services • Promoting transport and logistics solutions responsive to changing consumer demands • Developing centralized web portals as information hubs • Promoting coordinated border management	**Gender and Care Sector** • Assessment of adverse impacts of pandemic on gender • Knowledge sharing on issues of unpaid work, community-based care, long-term care, domestic workers, public and private affordable care for children and the elderly **Education and Labor Markets** • Knowledge sharing and capacity building on educational technologies • Coordination on labor market information systems • Harmonization of educational competencies and skills standards • Regional frameworks for mutual recognition of educational qualifications • Regional frameworks for online quality assurance and credentials	**Financial Inclusion** • Policy and regulatory cooperation on regional payment settlements • Digital payment schemes • Knowledge sharing, best-practice dissemination **Financial Safety Nets** • Strengthen frameworks for regional financing arrangements, macroeconomic and financial surveillance, and crisis assistance • Cooperation to tackle emerging issues on financial safety-net arrangements and to manage financial technology **Disaster Preparedness and Management** • Capacity building to strengthen coordination mechanisms and communications systems for pandemics
Deeper regional cooperation and integration	**Resilient Infrastructure** • Investments in resilient cross-border infrastructure (risk prevention, rapid recovery, data protection and safety, etc.) • Inclusivity for a wide range of users • Multimodal connectivity • Transport facilitation • Decarbonizing transport systems		**Trade Facilitation** • Joint actions on regulatory and institutional reforms based on international and regional framework agreements • Trade information portals • Monitoring of trade facilitation performance • Information sharing on best practices • Capacity building for implementing Trade Facilitation Agreement and Revised Kyoto Convention **Tourism** • Regional coordination in opening borders • Safe and seamless border management • Use of technology for safe, seamless, and touchless travel • Reliable, consistent, and easy access to information on travel restrictions and protocols • Harmonization of travel and tourism related health protocols • Promotion of low-carbon tourism • Travel facilitation	**Regional Health Security** • Soft components of healthcare delivery • Governance • Health finance • Cross-border registration of health workers and pooled training • Regional buffer stocking of essential medicines • Regional public goods for health **Social Protection** • Monitoring and reporting on social protection programs (Social Protection Index) • Knowledge sharing on new themes: new vulnerabilities created by COVID-19, fiscal limitations and long-term sustainability, linking of social protection to livelihood opportunities • Capacity building for multisectoral actors **Low-Carbon Transition** • Integrated solutions to low-carbon transition • Information sharing and benchmarking • Technological development and diffusion • Common standards for cross-border infrastructure	**Migration** • Shared information infrastructure and migrant registration • Dialogue on policy gaps in worker protection, risk mitigation for migrants • Common template on streamlined procedures to acquire portability of social protection • Knowledge sharing on best practices **Renewable Energy** • Regional trade in hydropower • Harmonization of technical, institutional frameworks, and tariff and/or pricing regimes • Dialogues on climate change impacts and social impacts associated with hydropower
More open regional cooperation and integration	**More open and flexible approaches that cut across or go beyond existing regional and subregional groupings** • Promotion of inter-subregional cooperation on transport and trade facilitation **More open platforms for policy dialogue, knowledge sharing, and capacity building** • Development of knowledge-sharing platforms such as the trade facilitation subgroup under the Regional Cooperation and Integration Committee • Use of the Regional Cooperation and Integration Community Site as an online platform for knowledge sharing and interdepartmental collaboration			**Better collaboration with development partners; expanded partnerships with think tanks, academic institutions, and civil society organizations** • Use of adaptation of guidelines and tool kits already developed by regional and international organizations • Promotion of sector and/or thematic regional cooperation and integration knowledge sharing among think tanks and subregional centers of excellence **Pooling of knowledge and resources for greater efficiency of access** • Distillation of key messages and findings in knowledge products to serve as inputs to the workings of subregional programs and regional platforms	

Source: Authors' adaptation from Asian Development Bank. 2019. *Strategy 2030 Operational Plan for Priority 7—Fostering Regional Cooperation and Integration 2019–2024*. Manila.

Regional cooperation platforms can help frame strategies and regulations, especially for cross-border data flows; streamline requirements across borders; and reduce regulatory impediments. The ability to move, store, and process data across borders is the foundation of the modern international data economy,[9] which countries must confront if they are to thrive in the post–COVID-19 recovery phase. However, countries can attract inbound data flows only when they have established a secure and transparent telecommunications infrastructure and regulatory framework, especially for data privacy and cybersecurity. Data flows will require trust between economies, based on their shared understanding and approach to managing their data economy and reducing risks. Regional cooperation can exploit technology dividends by making broadband infrastructure available in sparsely populated areas along the borders (last-mile connectivity). A regionally consistent framework for cross-border data flows can maximize the benefits from emerging technologies to build a data economy for a resilient recovery. Alignment with international standards and model laws such as from the United Nations (UN) Commission on International Trade Law will be essential since data flows are not confined to a region.

(ii) **E-commerce.** Key digital platform reforms can focus on the need for policies and regulations to manage market disruptions and unfair competition, innovation and creation of new products, access of micro businesses, and data privacy and cybersecurity. Policies will cover, among others, e-commerce infrastructure (i.e., telecommunications and network technologies); multimedia applications; electronic data interchange; database management; internet service providers; human computer interface; and digital literacy. Regional cooperation can harmonize regulatory and technical standards for data systems critical to integrating markets.[10] Capacity building can focus on digital solutions in areas such as education, health, transport and multimodal trade facilitation, and technology startup ecosystems. Regional cooperation can ease the transition to cross-border e-commerce by fast-tracking the implementation of e-commerce policies and reforms. Regional cooperation can help build and strengthen the capabilities of MSMEs affected by COVID-19 to recover and grow in the postpandemic period. A regional approach to raising finance for technology can support digital transformation in economies with limited access to finance. Development partners and multilateral institutions can play an important role in building the trust and confidence of public, private, and personal stakeholders in technological development.

Box 1 illustrates how CAREC is tackling new opportunities and challenges related to digitalization and e-commerce.

BOX 1

Digitalization and E-commerce

Under the Central Asia Regional Economic Cooperation (CAREC) 2030 Strategy, the integration of information and communication technology (ICT) across CAREC operations is a crosscutting priority. CAREC is, therefore, developing the CAREC Digital Strategy 2030 in alignment with CAREC 2030 and technological priorities of member countries. The strategy will promote measures to integrate ICT across CAREC operational clusters and ensure the continuity of other initiatives under CAREC 2030.

Source: Asian Development Bank. 2020. *Supporting Startup Ecosystem in the Central Asia Regional Economic Cooperation Region to Mitigate Impact of COVID-19 and Support Economic Revival.* Manila.

---

9   World Economic Forum. 2020. *A Roadmap for Cross-Border Data Flows. A White Paper.*
10   UN Economic and Social Commission for Asia and the Pacific (UNESCAP), ADB, UN Development Programme. 2021. *Responding to the COVID-19 Pandemic: Leaving No Country Behind.*

(iii) **Safe international mobility.** To cope with restrictions on international travel, governments, working with industry, have instituted border protocols covering testing, quarantine, and contact tracing. Although the responses at the onset of the COVID-19 emergency were limited and ad hoc, they gradually became more systematic and better coordinated. The Organisation for Economic Co-operation and Development has launched a safe international mobility initiative that could be a model for a similar initiative in Asia and the Pacific. The objective is to promote greater certainty, safety, and security in travel as countries reopen. Tourism, transport, health, immigration, and labor agencies can better understand the various protocols through a knowledge-sharing forum, which can be used to gauge the appetite for a comprehensive blueprint for safe international travel. Countries can collaborate on harmonizing practices for regional contact tracing with the use of digital tools, a system for classifying risks, vaccination certification requirement, mobile health insurance, protocols for testing travelers, and principles for generating electronic certificates for travel that ensure privacy protection and security.

Safe international mobility also covers the area of labor mobility, given the rapid expansion of labor markets beyond borders. Mobility of labor involves complex challenges in governance and migrant workers' protection that require regional and international cooperation. ASEAN has taken steps to ease regional mobility for skilled labor through mutual recognition agreements, which establish common skills and qualification recognition schemes. The Pacific labor mobility program focuses on seasonal workers (Australia) and seasonal employers (New Zealand) and considers the temporary migration programs alongside other migration pathways open to Pacific islanders in the region and other temporary migration programs globally.

(iv) **Resilient supply chains.** Governments will be looking for opportunities in emerging international production structures, while facing the challenges of increased divestment, relocation and diversion, and tougher competition for foreign direct investment. Regional supply chains will need to be mapped and opportunities to further strengthen them identified. Cross-border collaboration among public and private stakeholders will be key to ensuring that transport and logistics solutions will adequately respond to shifting consumer spending patterns and be tailored to potential accelerated growth in e-commerce. Mitigating supply chain disruption risks from natural hazards is another important area where countries can collaborate in scenario planning, stress testing, and understanding of the dynamic nature of risks. Information on trade procedures can be shared through centralized web portals. Regional bodies and institutions can continue to encourage supply chains by providing trade finance to support export credit insurers and allow banking institutions to finance small and medium-sized enterprises (Box 2).

BOX 2

Trade and Supply Chain Finance Program

The Asian Development Bank (ADB) Trade and Supply Chain Finance Program (TSCFP) fills market gaps in trade finance by providing guarantees and loans to banks. The TSCFP's supply chain finance business aims to reduce financing gaps faced by small and medium-sized enterprises (SMEs) to help them join the global trading system. From 2009 to 2020, out of 33,093 transactions supported by the program, 21,713 involved SMEs. Transactions in that period amounted to $47.5 billion, including $28.1 billion through cofinancing. Beginning in 2020, a $500 million import facility to help developing member countries purchase vaccines and related equipment was offered through the TSCFP. The facility is aligned with the criteria under ADB's Asia Pacific Vaccine Access Facility. Cofinancing with private sector partners could result in the import facility supporting $1 billion in vaccines and related imports within a year.

Sources: ADB. 2021. *Trade and Supply Chain Finance Program (TSCFP) Fact Sheet*; and ADB. Trade and Supply Chain Finance Program.

(v) **Gender and the care economy.** Women are among the most vulnerable to the pandemic because of their employment patterns and low wages. More women than men lost their jobs because of their concentration in vulnerable occupations, increased burden of unpaid work, and limited access to finance for their businesses.[11] Measures to resolve these issues will include policies to redistribute women's care responsibilities; increase women's labor force participation; create models of public and private high-quality affordable care for children, the elderly, and the disabled; improve conditions of female-dominated occupations; and support women's entrepreneurship through skills training and greater access to finance and technology.[12]

Effective intersectoral coordination among ministries will be essential to design policies and interventions for equity and inclusiveness while contributing to economic productivity. Although policies in these areas are mainly national, regional cooperation can help policy makers through knowledge sharing and capacity building on mainstreaming gender in various sectors, mobilizing domestic resources for gender equality, and designing health and social protection systems. Areas of focus can include (a) promoting women's access to and skills in trade (e-commerce) and tourism activities, (b) helping women in border communities participate in cross-border activities, (c) protecting migrant workers' benefits, and (d) enabling women-led MSMEs to join the cross-border supply chain and trade activities, among others.

(vi) **Education and labor markets.** Job creation, improved quality of work through new standards, and future-proof education will be important bridges to an inclusive and resilient economic recovery. Education will have to prioritize innovation, digital skills, and educational technology solutions to generate a potent workforce as multiple transitions between jobs become the norm. Upgrading education and labor market policies for an inclusive and resilient recovery must deal with emerging trends in workforce mobility across jobs and national borders made possible by digitalization and remote work, and with the need for reskilling and lifelong learning to cope with trends. Countries can collaborate on harmonizing education and skills standards to promote comparability and mutual recognition of educational qualifications that can expedite the cross-border mobility of education professionals, students, and skilled workers. A regional qualifications framework can be formulated—as has been done in ASEAN—to provide a common reference to compare education qualifications across participating states. ASEAN cooperation in education offers a good model for improving education through harmonization of standards, competency frameworks, quality assurance, and interprofessional collaboration and mobility.

(vii) **Financial inclusion.** Financial inclusion and the development of payment systems and transactions disrupted by COVID-19 are important to households and businesses, especially MSMEs. To foster financial inclusion, regulators must bring down the structural barriers impeding access to financial services and digitalization of financial transactions and innovations in financial technology (fintech), and promote financial literacy. Regional cooperation can support national initiatives on financial inclusion through knowledge sharing, dissemination of experiences, and exchange of information on international best practices and successful models. Regional cooperation is possible in regulatory governance, such as ASEAN's regional payment settlements infrastructure to benefit cross-border trade, remittances, and retail payments. The ASEAN Payment Policy Framework guides cross-border real-time retail payments across member states to build a more competitive economic bloc.[13] ASEAN has taken steps to establish interoperable quick response (QR) codes for payments to achieve cross-border real-time retail payments in the subregion by 2025.

---

11 The hard-hit sectors are accommodation and food services; wholesale and retail trade; real estate, business, and administrative activities; and manufacturing. ILO. 2020. *ILO Monitor: COVID-19 and the World of Work*. Fifth edition. Geneva.
12 Southeast Asia Development Solutions. 2021. 6 Ways to Foster Inclusive Recovery in the Wake of the Pandemic.
13 ASEAN. 2019. Joint Statement of the 5th ASEAN Finance Ministers' and Central Bank Governors' Meeting (AFMGM).

This innovative retail payment instrument will lower the cost of services and encourage the use of local currencies in settling cross-border transactions.[14]

(viii) **Financial safety nets.** Transnational risks have mounted because of increasing cross-border regional economic interdependence and financial transactions, which have been compounded recently by the COVID-19 pandemic. Because risks are increasingly complex, countries must pool their resources to build regional financial safety nets. During the 1997–1998 Asian financial crisis, the region's economies built strong institutional frameworks for regional financing and macroeconomic and financial surveillance, and bolstered crisis assistance and management to restore economic and financial stability. The initiatives included the ASEAN+3 Economic Review and Policy Dialogue, the Chiang Mai Initiative Multilateralization, the Asian Bond Markets Initiative, and the ASEAN+3 Macroeconomic Research Office, which have collectively reinforced the region's financial stability and capacity to respond to crises.[15] Current efforts at resilient recovery could build on the initiatives by reviewing and strengthening them, and by dealing with emerging issues on financial safety-net arrangements involving the regulatory environment, to manage fintech and safeguard financial stability, data flows, and taxation of the digital economy. The efforts could have implications for ADB's role in the regional financial safety-net architecture in Asia and the Pacific. Regional dialogue and cooperation on strengthening financial safety nets can help bolster Asia's resilient recovery in the pandemic's aftermath.

(ix) **Disaster preparedness and management.** Measures to prepare for disasters and minimize their effects on loss of life and property include predicting, preventing, and mitigating the impact of disasters on vulnerable populations, and responding to their consequences. A resilient recovery requires institutional capacity, effective decision-making, strong recovery-focused relationships among ministries, well-functioning planning and coordination mechanisms, and well-defined methods and procedures to ensure that recovery activities are adequately informed and supported. Multilateral development banks including ADB, UN specialized agencies, and regional organizations such as ASEAN are continuing to support disaster preparedness and management mechanisms (e.g., the regional disaster contingent financing mechanism in the Pacific Humanitarian Pathway on COVID-19), as well as capacity development focusing on hazard events such as floods, tsunamis, and transboundary haze.

National disaster recovery frameworks provide the structure and context for involvement of stakeholders in recovery planning and operations. RCI interventions for disaster preparedness and management need to align with national frameworks and, if the frameworks are inadequate, to develop capacity and governance structures to generate favorable outcomes and impacts. The ASEAN Agreement on Disaster Management and Emergency Response supports resilience recovery interventions largely aligned with DMCs' plans and strategies and has provided a model of a regional recovery framework focusing on the hardest-hit sectors. The CAREC Disaster Risk Transfer Facility is being developed to help countries mitigate risks from disasters arising from natural hazards and infectious disease outbreaks. The GMS COVID-19 Response Plan 2021–2023 has been prepared to respond to the medium-term health, economic, and social impacts of the pandemic and to complement the GMS-2030 Strategy.

---

[14] Malaysia's payment service infrastructure PayNet and Singapore's NETS officially launched real-time, cross-border debit card payments in late 2019. They are now collaborating to offer cross-border instant credit transfers and QR code payments between Singapore and Malaysia. The Bank of Thailand and the National Bank of Cambodia announced the launch of interoperable QR code payments that will allow Cambodian tourists in Thailand to pay for goods and services with their Cambodian digibank app. The amenity was developed as an overlay service on Thailand's PromptPay system. ACI Worldwide. 2020. Singapore and Malaysia Sow the Seeds for Cross-Border Success.

[15] ADB. 2019. *Strengthening Asia's Financial Safety Net*. Manila.

Deeper Regional Cooperation and Integration

(i) **Resilient infrastructure.** Cross-border infrastructure is particularly vulnerable to external threats because resilience policies and processes can differ widely between two or more countries. Dimensions of resilience run across the project life-cycle stages, from planning and design to construction, operations, and decommissioning. Elements of resilience include physical aspects, operations, data protection, and safety. Resilience as a process includes measures to anticipate and prevent risks, monitor performance, and mitigate the effects of failures when something goes wrong, allowing rapid recovery. Regional cooperation in infrastructure connectivity can be deepened by considering these dimensions. Understanding how infrastructure contributes to resilient communities is important, particularly in light of recovery efforts. Infrastructure has become increasingly complex, owing to the development issues of integrating across different sectors and thematic areas. In the case of transport, thematic areas for regional cooperation include multimodal connectivity, including maritime connectivity across subregions, transport facilitation, cross-border flow of goods and people, and inclusivity for a wide range of users and stakeholders.

(ii) **Trade facilitation.** At the onset of the COVID-19 emergency, governments were quick to initiate a wide array of trade facilitation measures to keep supply chains running while protecting workers at ports, terminals, and border-crossing points. The measures include (a) relaxation of border procedures, (b) risk management to prioritize clearance of imports and exports of low-risk critical supplies, (c) border agency cooperation to expedite the import of critical supplies, (d) increase of the availability of trade-related information on websites and through inquiry points, and (e) protection of frontline workers through social distancing and regular testing.[16] As Asia and the Pacific recovers, governments will continue to face challenges brought about by inherent weaknesses in the trade facilitation environment. Trade facilitation can leverage the exigencies of the pandemic to accelerate long-term regulatory and institutional reforms prescribed under international or regional framework agreements. The reforms include the development of electronic single windows, risk management, paperless trade through digitalization of customs and other trade facilitation procedures, and coordinated border management, among others. Although trade facilitation reform is fundamentally a domestic unilateral issue requiring political will, it can benefit from regional cooperation through its inclusion in subregional cooperation programs, implementation through policy dialogue, sharing of trade facilitation practices and knowledge as well as capacity building, expansion of trade information portals, development of regional electronic single windows, and benchmarking and monitoring of trade facilitation performance (Box 3).

(iii) **Tourism.** The resumption of tourism will likely see the following trends: (a) preference for domestic or proximity tourism, (b) increasing emphasis on health and hygiene, and (c) increased demand for environmentally sustainable tourism. Regional cooperation can play an important role in coordinating the reopening of borders for safe and seamless passage. Tourism corridors or travel bubbles could be a starting point. Initiatives could focus on harmonized travel and tourism-related protocols at the border, standardization and/or mutual recognition of digital vaccine certificates and travel passes, coordinated border management, and travel facilitation. Countries can collaborate on (a) developing reliable, consistent, and easy access to information, including health protocols and access to medical services and facilities; and (b) policies and programs that support benefit sharing with local communities and job creation. Joint capacity building will be helpful in keeping the quality of tourism services up to a set standard. Training tourism professionals and workers in digital technologies will be particularly useful to cater to tourists'

---

[16] S. Sela, A. Yang, and M. Zawacki. 2020. *Trade Facilitation Best Practices Implemented in Response to the COVID-19 Pandemic. Trade and COVID-19 Guidance Note.* Washington, DC: World Bank.

BOX 3

Trade Facilitation

Trade facilitation is a key strategic priority of the South Asian Subregional Economic Cooperation (SASEC) Program. The SASEC Operational Plan 2016–2025 aims to broaden the scope of transport and trade facilitation measures and logistics development to synchronize with infrastructure investments across intermodal transport routes. Trade facilitation initiatives cover land and sea routes to support efficient distribution and collection of goods at intermodal hubs. The Asian Development Bank is conducting a midterm review of the SASEC Vision. The review is expected to expand the scope of SASEC's trade facilitation agenda and will likely include a shift in focus to supply chain mapping and logistics.

Source: Asian Development Bank. 2016. *South Asia Subregional Economic Cooperation Operational Plan 2016–2025.* Manila.

---

requirements. The emerging trend of proximity tourism offers opportunities to develop tourism packages for intraregional travel accompanied by marketing campaigns to visit the subregion as a single destination.

(iv) **Regional health security.** The COVID-19 pandemic has accentuated the urgency of strengthening health systems in Asia and the Pacific, which is prone to emerging and reemerging infectious diseases. Regional health security requires a multisectoral and multi-stakeholder approach encompassing a wide range of measures. Under the One Health approach, and in the context of sustainable economic recovery, regional health security will need to be strengthened in (a) the soft components of health service delivery, including digital health; (b) governance (institutions, regulations, and accreditation); (c) health finance; and (d) regional public goods for health. Regional cooperation will be vital in setting up regional surveillance, reporting and disease management policies, and governance processes that operate seamlessly across national borders (Box 4). Investing in surge capacity will foster resiliency of regional health security systems, which includes preparedness of the health system's workforce (including pooled training), cross-border registration of health workers, and building regional buffer stocks of key essential medicines (footnote 10).

BOX 4

Regional Health Security

The Greater Mekong Subregion (GMS) Health Cooperation Strategy 2019–2023 provides a framework for collective efforts to tackle health issues. Regional cooperation focuses on (i) improved GMS health system response to public health threats, (ii) strengthened protection of vulnerable communities from the health impacts of regional integration, and (iii) greater human resource capacity to respond to priority health issues in GMS. The GMS Health Security Project will strengthen their responses to emerging infectious diseases and the management of other major public health threats, manage weaknesses in the countries' health systems, and promote cross-country cooperation to improve national and international health security.

Sources: ADB. 2019. *Greater Mekong Subregion Health Cooperation Strategy 2019–2023.* Manila; and ADB. Greater Mekong Subregion Health Security Project.

(v)   **Social protection.** Social protection is central to inclusive and resilient recovery. COVID-19 has triggered an unprecedented response from governments in the form of noncontributory cash transfers, expanded health benefits, and unemployment insurance. In many cases, the responses are ad hoc and short-term, and reflect a lack of effective and adequate social protection systems. An important regional initiative on social protection was launched by the UN Economic and Social Commission for Asia and the Pacific (UNESCAP) in October 2020: Action Plan to Strengthen Regional Cooperation on Social Protection in Asia and the Pacific, which defines the regional shared vision and strategy and a set of national actions to be implemented on a voluntary basis by 2030.[17] Universal social protection and the Social Protection Floor Initiative are among the salient features of the plan. ADB has developed a strong portfolio on social protection focusing on key areas such as digitalization (including identification and registration, payments, monitoring); portability; and adaptive and shock-responsive programs. ADB has provided regional technical assistance to enable Pacific island countries to meet their distinct needs for social insurance, social assistance, and active labor market programs. Regional knowledge sharing on good practices is essential for rapid adoption of good practices.

The portability of social protection is critical for safe and secure cross-labor mobility. Despite the considerable economic impact of labor migration on individuals, households, and countries of destination, the social protection afforded to migrant workers and their families is generally weak, partly as a result of inadequate provision in national policy frameworks and legal systems, and because of the absence of applicable bilateral arrangements. Streamlined and coherent responses will require national, regional, and multilateral coordination of immigration, labor, and social security legal and policy frameworks and administrative practices to build a system of regional governance for social protection. Social protection and the issue of portability have been an important item on the ASEAN agenda but progress has been slow and limited to bilateral initiatives.

(vi)   **Migration.** Migrants face greater risks in times of crises because they generally lack social protection and access to health care and other essential services. Although migration policies are national, governments can benefit from external advice and knowledge of best practices through regional cooperation. Opportunities for regional cooperation include (a) establishing common infrastructure for sharing accurate, relevant, and timely migrant-related information and best practices to support policy making and migrant registration; (b) implementing policies on remittances and the cost of cross-border transactions; (c) bridging policy gaps or strengthening enforcement of existing worker protection frameworks in destination countries; (d) conducting policy dialogues or other forms of collective action to help identify solutions to manage the flow of people across borders and to mitigate heightened risks for migrants; and (e) establishing national protection frameworks based on a common template and coordinated streamlined procedures to acquire portability of social protection or access to new resources.

(vii)   **Renewable energy.** Governments have put policies in place to transition to a low-carbon economy by increasing access to clean and renewable energy, scaling up the deployment of renewable energy, and improving demand-side efficiency. ADB-supported subregional programs have prioritized cooperation in renewable energy, focusing on regional trade in hydropower. These platforms have proven effective in advancing discussions on technical, institutional, and tariff and pricing issues; complex environmental, climate change impacts; and the social drawbacks usually associated with hydropower generation. Well-planned hydropower projects can help supply sustainable energy but need proper planning, careful system design, and adaptation measures to manage the challenges. Energy planners, investors, and other

---

[17] UNESCAP. 2020. *Action Plan to Strengthen Regional Cooperation on Social Protection in Asia and the Pacific*. Bangkok.

stakeholders can benefit from RCI in exchanging up-to-date knowledge and information to make informed decisions on hydropower projects.

(viii) **Climate change and low-carbon transition.** As economies recover, policies for a low-carbon transition that started before the pandemic should be intensified and mainstreamed into recovery plans. Accelerating the low-carbon transition will require concerted efforts and harmonized actions to achieve the SDGs and the Paris Agreement commitments. Countries can leverage the recovery process to have more ambitious nationally determined contributions to attain the net-zero goal by the middle of this century. Regional cooperation will need to step up in developing integrated solutions, directly promoting regional mitigation by sharing information and benchmarking; collaborating on technology development and diffusion; setting and implementing common standards on sustainable border infrastructure; and promoting trade in renewable energy, among others. ADB will help its DMCs produce road maps to guide policies and strategies for accelerated low-carbon transition (Box 5), including for nationally determined contributions. An emerging issue that will figure prominently in regional dialogues is the plan by the European Union, supported by the United States, to impose a tax on the carbon content of imports. The plan has intensified the debate on the use of trade for environmental ends; the potential use of the carbon tax as a tool for domestic protection; and whether mitigation goals could be better achieved by directing interventions at the source (e.g., phasing out subsidies for fossils fuels) rather than through proxies.

BOX 5

Low-Carbon Transition

Many Pacific island countries are implementing plans to run on 100% renewables by transitioning to cleaner, more efficient power, which will decrease dependency on imported fossil fuels, increase access to affordable and reliable electricity, and reduce carbon dioxide emissions. The Asian Development Bank (ADB) is supporting the transition by providing finance and direct technical assistance. In 2019, ADB approved an umbrella facility of up to $100 million, which will provide financing support, including loans, guarantees, and letters of credit to overcome constraints on private sector investment in renewable power projects. The program aims to encourage private sector investment through an innovative blend of ADB direct private sector lending, ADB guarantees of commercial bank lenders, and donor funds that provide a backstop to payment obligations of power utilities. ADB is the largest investor in the Pacific island countries, and the program will leverage ADB's extensive network with power utilities to identify planned transactions in the early stages under the One ADB approach. The development of a regional guarantee program is an output indicator of the Pacific Renewable Energy Investment Facility, which was designed to support ADB investment in sovereign renewable energy projects in the smallest 11 Pacific developing member countries and to assist in sector reform. Technical assistance for projects under the program will strengthen governance and institutional capacity by building skills in financial sustainability, service delivery, transparent tender processes, and environmental and social standards.

Sources: ADB. 2021. *Pacific Renewable Energy Program Interim Review Report*. Manila; ADB. 2019. ADB Investing Over $1 Billion to Help Pacific's Renewable Energy Transition. News release. 1 December; ADB. 2019. ADB Approves New Financing Support for Renewable Power Projects in the Pacific. News release. 23 April; and ADB. Pacific Renewable Energy Program.

More Open Regional Cooperation and Integration

(i) **More open and flexible approaches that cut across or go beyond existing regional and subregional groupings.** More open RCI could expand project development and policy dialogue geographically, transcending subregional boundaries and involving existing and emerging areas of cooperation. Ongoing work on promoting inter-subregional cooperation on transport, especially maritime connectivity, and trade facilitation between South Asia and Southeast Asia may be expanded to cover other areas, such as power trade, tourism, and migration. Promoting Central Asia–South Asia cooperation may be considered.

(ii) **More open platforms for policy dialogue, knowledge sharing, and capacity building.** Knowledge sharing on common, priority cross-subregional challenges and opportunities such as digital trade, trade facilitation, or migration would be helpful starting points to initiate cross-subregional project development work. Efforts to strengthen interdepartmental collaboration on trade facilitation are already underway, beginning with the formation in ADB of the Trade Facilitation Subgroup under the RCI Thematic Group. The subgroup will be responsible for increasing knowledge sharing, augmenting support for operations, expanding coordination and advocacy, and developing trade facilitation strategies and frameworks on trade facilitation-related matters. The ADB RCI Community Site on SharePoint can be utilized more fully as a virtual space for discussions and engagement to make it more community-driven. A unifying communication framework or strategy will be needed, focused on users' needs and fully supported by the RCI Committee.

(iii) **Stronger collaboration with development partners.** This includes expanded partnerships with think tanks, academic institutions, and civil society organizations.

Using or adapting guidelines and tool kits already developed by regional and international organizations will be a valuable form of knowledge partnership. Examples are UNESCAP's Asia-Pacific E-Resilience Toolkit, Web-Toolkit for Integrated Planning of Infrastructure Corridors, and the Readiness Assessment Guide for Cross-border Paperless Trade. The World Bank has developed the Digital Development Toolkits Series to help users (a) identify challenges and necessary policy and regulatory actions in digital development, (b) analyze potential solutions, and (c) provide practical examples from countries that have resolved digital development-related matters. The tool kits include the Broadband Strategies Toolkit, the Cross-Sector Infrastructure Sharing Toolkit, the Cloud Readiness Assessment Toolkit, the Engendering ICT Toolkit, the Digital Government Readiness Assessment Toolkit, the Digital Capabilities Knowledge Map, and the Digital Capability Framework. The World Customs Organization has developed several tool kits on modernizing customs. The tool kits can be used by countries for self-assessment, with ADB building on them to incorporate regional dimensions. The development of regional tool kits is one area where ADB can add significant value in collaboration with regional and international organizations. Self-assessments will promote greater country ownership (especially for implementing agencies) and help countries internalize their own needs and policy actions, thus building capacity. ADB's role will be to ease the process in collaboration with development partners.

Sector and thematic RCI knowledge sharing among think tanks and subregional centers of excellence can stimulate innovation and applied learning as well as fill in knowledge and/or skills gaps. The ADB–Asian Think Tanks Network serves as a platform for members to exchange views, discuss research work, and share experiences on pressing development concerns.[18] Since 2013, six forums have been held on

---

18 The ADB–Asian Think Tanks Network is an informal group of think tanks engaged in research on sustainable growth and inclusive development in Asia and the Pacific. It has about 40 member institutions based in ADB member countries, mainly state economic development policy research institutions.

topics such as (a) innovation and inclusion, (b) financing sustainable urbanization, and (c) technology and human capital development.

(iv) **Pooling knowledge and resources for greater efficiency of access.** Regional and international agencies are continuously developing knowledge products to support decision-makers at the policy, program, and project levels. For instance, three new strategic knowledge products on RCI's role in a post–COVID-19 environment in Asia and the Pacific were produced by ADB, UNESCAP, and United Nations Development Programme in the later part of 2020 and the first half of 2021: (i) *Asian Economic Integration Report: Making Digital Platforms Work for Asia and the Pacific*; (ii) *Future of Regional Cooperation in Asia and the Pacific*; and (iii) *Responding to the COVID-19 Pandemic: Leaving No Country Behind.*[19] Each document analyzes in depth particular development trends and issues and discusses the role of RCI in tackling them to achieve national and regional objectives and the SDGs. The challenge is to distill and communicate the knowledge products' key messages and findings to subregional programs and regional platforms to deepen and expand the perspectives of decision-makers and stakeholders on vital issues.

[19] ADB. 2021. *Asian Economic Integration Report: Making Digital Platforms Work for Asia and the Pacific.* Manila; ADB. 2020. *Future of Regional Cooperation in Asia and the Pacific.* Manila; and United Nations Development Program. 2021. Responding to the COVID-19 Pandemic: Leaving No Country Behind.

Cushioning the pandemic's impact on MSMEs, the poor, and the vulnerable. ADB-supported subregional platforms can facilitate dialogue on economic recovery, such as how to expand the market of women entrepreneurs (photo by Achmad Ibrahim).

5 Guiding Principles

The following principles can guide the use of the wider, deeper, and more open RCI framework for post-COVID-19 recovery.

(i) **Regional cooperation and integration interventions need to be more mindful of the unique circumstances of countries participating in an RCI initiative.** Regional cooperation will only be as strong as its weakest link. Recognizing the weakest link and providing additional or customized interventions to overcome its handicaps will ensure that the weakest country is not disproportionately disadvantaged in receiving the full benefits of a regional cooperation project. The long-term goal is for ADB to ensure that all countries in the region can participate fully and meaningfully in the evolving RCI environment and that no country is left behind on account of the fluidity and accelerated pace of events. As advisor, knowledge provider, and capacity builder, ADB should be more discerning of countries' special needs and circumstances—such as those of small island developing states, fragile and conflict-affected states, and landlocked economies—and provide customized approaches aligned with national plans and priorities. RCI platforms can be used to shore up weak and lagging countries so that they can reap the full benefits of regional cooperation. As secretariat of key subregional cooperation programs, ADB can start the required analytical work, pool efforts and resources, and harness experiences and capacities from less affected and advanced economies to help their neighbors.

(ii) **The integrity of existing subregional programs should not be compromised by more open RCI, which will make institutional boundaries more permeable.** Under existing arrangements, all ADB-supported subregional programs operate under the 2+x principles, where any two countries can agree to cooperate on a project. Under the concept of more open RCI, the same principle can apply where two or more countries belonging to different subregional programs agree to collaborate. Such collaboration should be seen as an opportunity to strengthen and improve existing frameworks rather than diminish them. Collaboration should be project-based and timebound and avoid formal and permanent institutional frameworks unless a mechanism is needed to implement the project (e.g., a project implementation team).

(iii) **Country ownership and commitment are even more important.** Country ownership is seen in RCI initiatives and projects that are anchored in national development plans and public investment programs. However, the crafting of policies and reforms as part of the transition to recovery will be challenging, given continued uncertainties, heightened risks, and difficult trade-offs. To foster country ownership, ADB will need to guide national recovery by using evidence-based policy advice to optimize the benefits of RCI in complementing the plans.

(iv) **Regional cooperation and integration initiatives must align more closely with global agendas (e.g., SDGs, the Paris Agreement) to make them sustainable.** Regional cooperation can help countries meet their commitments to major global frameworks through harmonized actions. Countries should be encouraged to use self-assessment tool kits, templates, and models developed by multilateral development banks, UN specialized agencies, and other international organizations to help establish baselines from which they can develop pathways to meeting their global commitments. Regional cooperation in the form of dialogue, knowledge sharing, and capacity building can be initiated where it can complement or accelerate national efforts.

(v) **Innovative institutional arrangements under existing ADB-supported subregional frameworks should be encouraged.** Structural rigidities should give way to more innovative and responsive institutional arrangements so that RCI processes can transform into a culture of inclusiveness and openness. Some arrangements may include (a) expanded senior officials' meetings involving representatives from various ministries and agencies led by and/or coordinated by the nodal or focal ministry, instead of individual meetings of sector working groups; (b) working groups organized around a theme or program instead of a sector, with a diverse composition that reflects multisectoral and multi-stakeholder representation from government, businesses, academic institutions and think tanks, and communities; (c) program-based senior officials' meetings where representation is based on technical competence and specific mandates needed to expedite decision-making, problem resolution, and more efficient implementation of a program or project (e.g., senior officials' meeting for One Health); and (d) modular learning events organized based on specific needs (e.g., the level of e-commerce readiness in ICT capability, technology environment, and web presence). The idea is to challenge existing subregional programs to innovate new arrangements that work better in the evolving RCI environment.

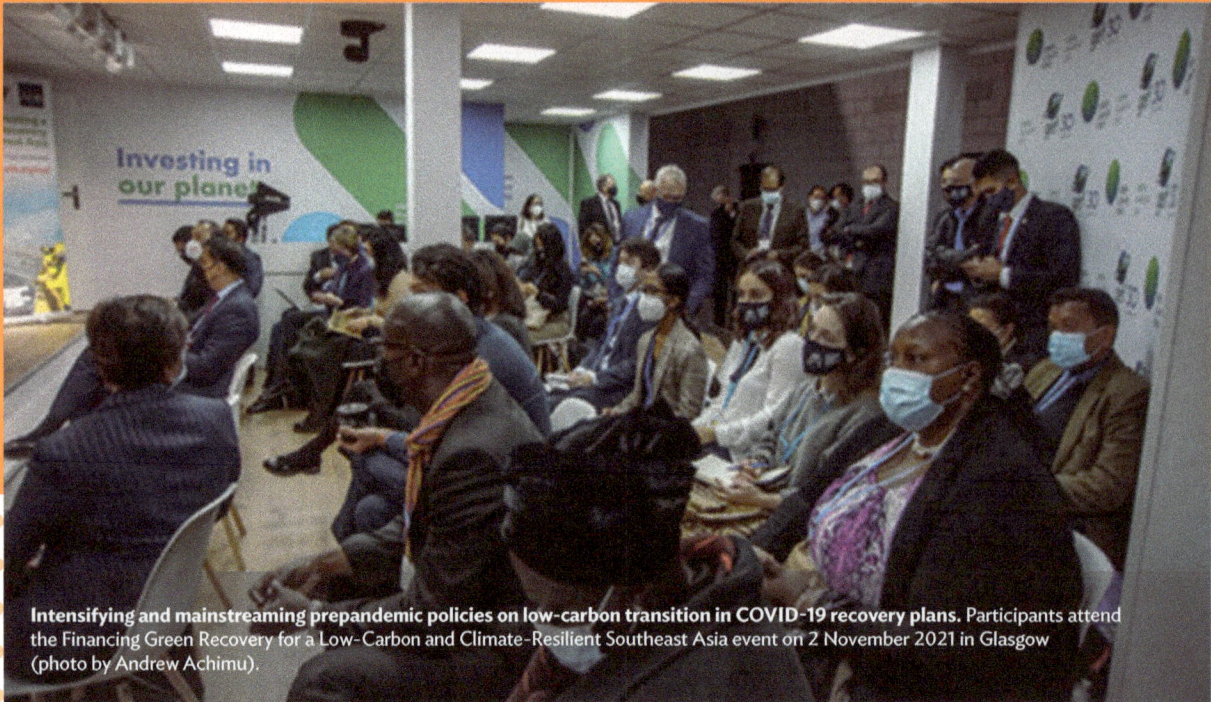

Intensifying and mainstreaming prepandemic policies on low-carbon transition in COVID-19 recovery plans. Participants attend the Financing Green Recovery for a Low-Carbon and Climate-Resilient Southeast Asia event on 2 November 2021 in Glasgow (photo by Andrew Achimu).

6 Implications for ADB's Institutional Support and Role in Regional Cooperation and Integration

Wider, deeper, and more open RCI will require stronger ADB institutional support and engagement with DMCs, the private sector, and development partners.

(i) **Wider and deeper RCI policy agenda.** The new development challenges resulting from the COVID-19 pandemic will require not only new investments but also new approaches to developing cross-border policies. Inequality between and within countries will become a greater focus of policy discourse among RCI planners in DMCs, including as part of subregional cooperation platforms, and in policy dialogue between DMCs and their development partners. Dialogue on policy cooperation and/or coordination to ensure an orderly exit from the pandemic, induced monetary and fiscal policies, regional cooperation in financial regulation, and financial safety net arrangements to safeguard financial stability will be among the core items in the policy agenda. The outcomes of the engagements will be reflected in individual RCI policy reforms and RCI program and project design and monitoring.

(ii) **Wider and deeper engagement with countries and stakeholders participating in RCI.** The complexity of development issues emerging from COVID-19 will require more intensive engagements with countries involved in RCI initiatives to ensure the responsiveness of ADB assistance to transition paths and recovery strategies. The multisectoral nature of most emerging issues will involve engaging with a wider set of stakeholders, which could affect the pace and quality of project planning, design, and implementation.

Widening and deepening RCI operations will have implications for ADB's roles as honest broker, knowledge provider and capacity builder, and finance mobilizer. As an honest broker, ADB is a regional advisor and/or secretariat to subregional programs. ADB will have to navigate a more complex and rapidly evolving landscape in helping participating countries find common ground as they recover. The analytical and diagnostic work that is the basis of ADB's impartial and reliable advice will have to be more attuned to the specific circumstances of participating countries and the possible emergence of new groupings. Improvements in cataloging and curating knowledge products, including the possible use of technology such as artificial intelligence, will be needed to ease access to and avoid duplication in producing knowledge products. Such improvements will help ADB formulate more timely and responsive interventions. Closer collaboration between ADB's regional departments and with knowledge departments will be needed. Although the ADB secretariat for each subregional program is lodged in a division in a regional department, it can draw on the wide range of expertise available in ADB to craft development solutions.

The current mainstream use of digital technology can create virtual spaces for regional knowledge sharing and capacity building that were not possible before. Digital technology can reinforce ADB's role as knowledge provider and capacity builder by enlarging learning spaces, thus increasing the benefits of shared knowledge as a regional public good without any significant incremental cost. Learning events organized by ADB or its subregional programs can be open to participation by other subregional programs. Greater awareness can open opportunities for inter-subregional program initiatives or for any group of countries that see the benefits of moving ahead on specific development challenges outside an existing subregional grouping.[20] Inter-subregional cooperation has been seen through an institutional lens (e.g., GMS and SASEC as collective groupings agreeing formally to collaborate). This institutional approach has the advantage of utilizing existing frameworks as the basis for collaboration but can be limiting given the diversity of development interests, priorities, and capacities within a subregional grouping. Virtual spaces will allow RCI to evolve with more fluidity and flexibility among countries with shared concerns and priorities. ADB should be able to seize the opportunity to foster wider, deeper, and more open RCI.

The role of ADB as mobilizer of development finance will need to be more proactive in developing innovative financial instruments, including those involving private sector engagement, to help accelerate recovery. At the start of the emergency, ADB developed the COVID-19 Pandemic Response Option as a countercyclical support instrument to prop up strained government budgets. ADB provided liquidity and working capital to the private sector through trade and supply chain finance. ADB developed theme bonds for gender, water, and health to support projects that contribute to sustainable growth in developing Asia, which are also being utilized to help combat the pandemic's impacts. Water bonds support projects under the Water Financing Program and highlight ADB's efforts to meet water sanitation needs. Health bonds finance ADB health projects. Gender bonds finance projects that promote gender equality and women's empowerment. The projects funded by theme bonds are aligned with the Sustainable Development Goals.

---

[20] For example, webinar breakout groups can be based on criteria other than geography or subregional grouping, e.g., gender gaps, service trade restrictiveness, and e-commerce readiness. Interactions among countries along thematic lines can broaden perspectives and catalyze innovative approaches to collaboration outside existing subregional frameworks.

Wider, deeper, and more open RCI opens more diverse opportunities for partnerships in finance, knowledge, and expertise. Given the magnitude of resources required for postpandemic recovery, engagement with development partners needs to be more strategic, i.e., focused on areas critical to recovery, where risks need to be mitigated and the chances of success increased. Strategic partnerships can revolve around (i) sustainability-themed funds; (ii) financing of regional and international public goods essential to recovery (e.g., inclusive and accessible health, educational technology); (iii) alignment of finance with the SDGs; (iv) support to public financing policies and programs that promote jobs and shore up incomes, especially for vulnerable groups; and (v) support to private sector environmental, social, and governance–linked investments.

The potential for expanded RCI operations will open more opportunities for ADB to use the full suite of its assistance modalities. ADB's RCI investment operations are mainly conventional project loans and grants. RCI-related policy-based lending (about 16%) is notable, but below the corporate-wide share permitted by ADB. Results-based lending is generally less than 2% but involves economic and social sectors. RCI operations can be expanded alongside the private sector. Nonsovereign RCI lending in 2016–2019 amounted to $1.3 billion, covering 18 projects concentrated in four sectors. An expanded RCI agenda can significantly increase the volume and number of RCI operations that involve private sector participation, including public–private partnerships and nonsovereign operations.

Some strategic opportunities that may be explored include (i) investments in quality infrastructure in accordance with international standards (i.e., the G20 Principles for Quality Infrastructure Investment) to meet medium- to long-term needs, including in telecommunications and finance; (ii) SDG-oriented regional investment cooperation supported by a regional compact or agreement; (iii) alignment with private sector finance (e.g., business or investment climate, upgrading of MSMEs) to develop new forms of partnership and tools for opportunity and risk sharing; (iv) calls for private investment in international public goods to help provide a global response to the COVID-19 pandemic (e.g., research on a vaccine and/or treatment, development of more effective tests, sharing of best practices) and in areas essential to sustainable and resilient recovery (educational technology, low-carbon transition, decent jobs).[21]

---

[21] United Nations. 2020. *Financing for Development in the Era of COVID-19 and Beyond. Menu of Options for the Consideration of Heads of State and Government. Part II.*

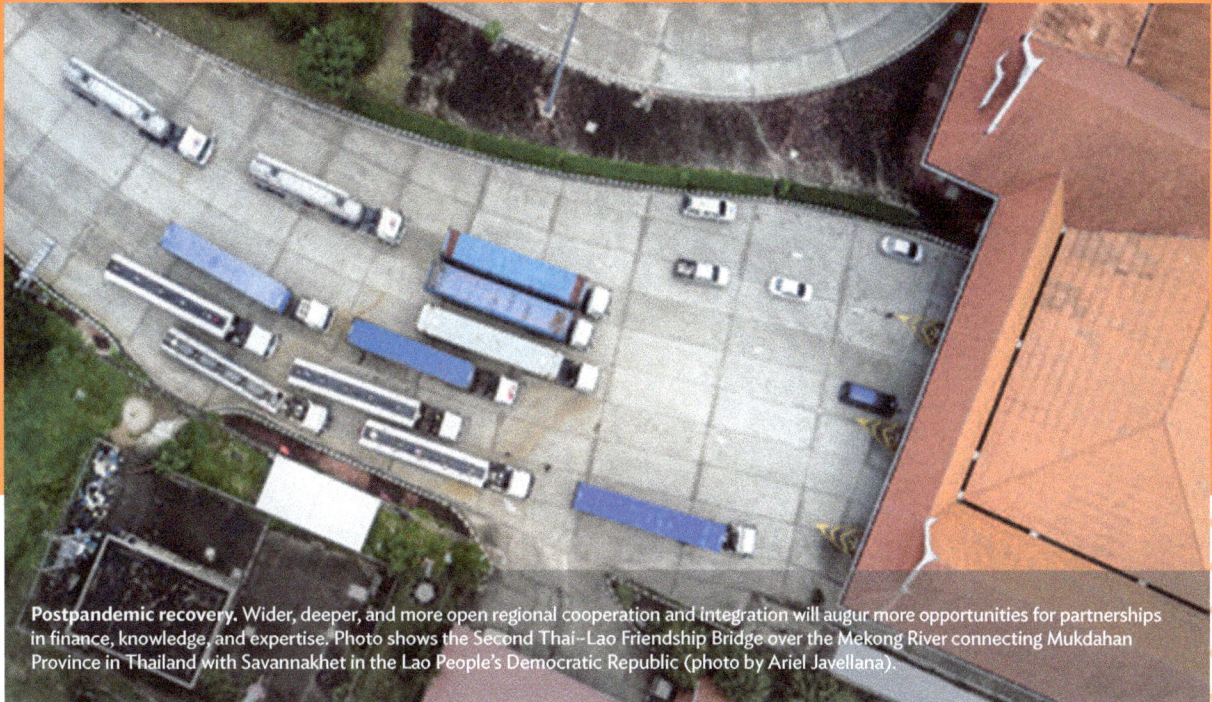

Postpandemic recovery. Wider, deeper, and more open regional cooperation and integration will augur more opportunities for partnerships in finance, knowledge, and expertise. Photo shows the Second Thai–Lao Friendship Bridge over the Mekong River connecting Mukdahan Province in Thailand with Savannakhet in the Lao People's Democratic Republic (photo by Ariel Javellana).

7 Conclusion

Recovery in the aftermath of the COVID-19 pandemic faces lingering uncertainties, heightened risks, and difficult trade-offs. It also opens many opportunities for countries to cooperate on coping with the challenges. ADB will need to be at the forefront of the recovery process to help countries rebuild smartly and open the pathways to an inclusive, resilient, and sustainable world. To be effective in this new environment, RCI will need to transform by widening its reach, deepening its engagement, and becoming more open to new processes and working arrangements.

This guidance note provides a broad framework and identifies opportunities—albeit indicative and not exhaustive—for fostering an inclusive, sustainable, and resilient postpandemic recovery where RCI can supplement or complement national efforts, leveraging the experience of past and ongoing initiatives. Many of these opportunities are in various stages of being developed or pursued by ADB through various platforms and mechanisms as an honest broker, knowledge provider, capacity builder, and mobilizer of development finance. The resources required to carry the recovery forward will be massive, requiring strategic partnerships, including with the private sector and development partners, to leverage strengths, distribute risks, and generate meaningful and rewarding outcomes. The guidance note helps DMCs to identify mutually beneficial initiatives in their transition to recovery; development partners to harness the potential for operational complementarity; and the private sector to contribute to innovations in finance, knowledge, and practice. For ADB's operations departments, the guidance note can further sharpen the strategies, focus, and approaches of their RCI operations and country program strategies to achieve inclusive, resilient, and sustainable recovery.

www.ingramcontent.com/pod-product-compliance
Lightning Source LLC
Chambersburg PA
CBHW050058220326
41599CB00045B/7459